The One Abiding

Books by Frederick Morgan

POETRY

The One Abiding, 2003

The Night Sky,
with photographs by Gaylen Morgan, 2002

Poems for Paula, 1995

Poems: New and Selected, 1987

Eleven Poems, 1983

Northbook, 1982

Refractions, 1981

Seven Poems by Mallarmé,
with images by Christopher Wilmarth, 1981

The River, 1980

Death Mother and Other Poems, 1979

Poems of the Two Worlds, 1977

A Book of Change, 1972

PROSE

The Fountain and Other Fables, 1985

The Tarot of Cornelius Agrippa, 1978

EDITOR

The Modern Image, 1965

The Hudson Review Anthology, 1961

THE ONE
ABIDING

Frederick Morgan

Introduction by Dana Gioia

Story Line Press
Ashland, Oregon

© 2003 by Frederick Morgan

First Printing

Published by Story Line Press, Three Oaks Farm,
P.O. Box 1240, Ashland, OR 97520-0055,
www.storylinepress.com.

This publication was made possible thanks
in part to the generous support of the
Nicholas Roerich Museum and our
individual contributors.

Author photo by Gaylen Morgan
Cover design by Lysa McDowell
Interior design and composition by
Valerie Brewster, Scribe Typography

LIBRARY OF CONGRESS
CATALOGING-IN-PUBLICATION DATA
Morgan, Frederick, 1922–
The one abiding / by Frederick Morgan.
p. cm.
ISBN 1-58654-021-1
I. Title.
PS3563.O83 O54 2003
811'.54—DC21
2002007754

For Paula as always

CONTENTS

xi   *Introduction: The Three Lives of*
Frederick Morgan

I

5   Washington Square

9   Eleventh Street

10   From the Guest Room Window

11   The Refuge

12   The Christmas Tree

13   The Clock

14   1932

II

19   May Night

20   Dolores

22   September 1957

23   Gifts

24   "You stirred so gently on the bed . . ."

25   The Recreant

26   The Parting

III

29   Anaktoria

30   "I called up Myrtis from the dead . . ."

31   Actaeon

32   Pasiphaë

33   Hypatia

35   In The Private Hospital

37   The Tower

IV

41 The Sign
44 The Burial
45 The Return
46 The Friend
47 The Shamrock
48 The Body
50 Recollections of Japan
53 Meditation at Sundown

V

59 The Watcher
60 A Dream
61 The Priest
63 Nothing
64 Rain
65 "When I awoke at last . . ."
67 After Shen Zhou

69 *A Note on the Author*
70 *Acknowledgments*

INTRODUCTION:
THE THREE LIVES OF
FREDERICK MORGAN

by Dana Gioia

Most American literati know about the two lives of Frederick Morgan —his two public lives, that is, the editor and the poet. These two active, distinguished, and somewhat overlapping careers mark him as one of the major American men of letters of the past half century. Of these two lives, his role as editor is surely better known. For fifty years Frederick Morgan was the editor of *The Hudson Review*, the greatest postwar quarterly in U.S. literature.

The history of this remarkably dynamic and independent-minded quarterly deserves its own careful account. Under Morgan's watch, *The Hudson Review* published writers as important and diverse as T.S. Eliot, Wallace Stevens, Ezra Pound, William Carlos Williams, Allen Tate, Anthony Hecht, Sylvia Plath, Anne Sexton, W.S. Merwin, Wendell Berry, A.R. Ammons, Louis Simpson, William Stafford, and Dylan Thomas, to name only a few of the poets and skip over the scores of fiction writers, essayists, philosophers, and cultural critics who have graced the journal's pages. As he has always reminded critics and journalists, Morgan usually had partners in *The Hudson Review*. He co-founded the journal in 1948 with two fellow Princetonians—his classmate Joseph Bennett and the slightly younger William Arrowsmith. (Arrowsmith left the editorial triumvirate in 1960, and Bennett died in 1972.) And for nearly a quarter century until his retirement in 1998, Morgan shared the editorship with his wife, Paula Deitz, who now serves as sole editor-in-chief.

It is no secret, however, that for the fifty years of his tenure, Morgan was the *Hudson*'s central guiding intelligence, the prime mover who created, developed, and sustained a major cultural enterprise. Most famous quarterlies have ten years of great influence and cultural prominence before settling into a steady, predictable routine. Great journals like *Kenyon Review* or *Partisan Review* articulate and critique the issues of a particular period so powerfully that they often become frozen in their own successful identity, which becomes less relevant with each passing year. Morgan kept *The Hudson Review* uniquely fresh, alert, and consistently pertinent by subtly reinventing it each decade to address the changing needs of American culture, often bringing a new generation of writers into the journal without losing the best of his established older contributors. *The Hudson Review* has enjoyed over half a century of uninterrupted excellence and influence, and the reason is mostly Frederick Morgan's high standards, flexible style, and visionary guidance. There is probably no more distinguished literary editor alive in America—and few equals. Ironically, that singular accomplishment has been no small burden for his alternate identity as poet.

Among literati Morgan's second public life is hardly less well known, but it remains—for a variety of reasons—less well understood. He has been widely recognized and often honored as a poet, but in sharp contrast to the public recognition of his editorial achievements, the considerable, indeed singular, accomplishments of his poetry have not yet been either properly placed or adequately evaluated. For his many admirers, this situation has been both puzzling and frustrating. And his admirers are numerous, especially among his fellow poets. Substantial appreciations of his work have been published by writers as diverse as Guy Davenport, Hayden Carruth, Sydney Lea, Alfred Corn, Richard Tillinghast, Emily Grosholz, Louis Simpson, and R.S. Gwynn. Although unanimous in their praise, the many individual tributes—including my own early assessment—have not yet created a critical consensus on his work. It seems not only fair to say, but virtually unavoidable to observe, that Morgan's poetic achievement has utterly outstripped all critical accounts of it. His individual volumes of poetry have been discussed intelligently and favorably, but there is not yet either an adequate appreciation or even cogent description of his total poetic career. His work has never been convincingly placed in relation to his contemporaries or explained in relation to its own complex variety.

Why would a poet who has had every stage of his career discussed intelligently by some of the most articulate poet-critics of the period currently exist in a critical vacuum? Is his work, so seemingly direct, somehow covertly dense or obscure? Does his wide-ranging poetry lack any identifiable center, but exist only as a collection of isolated achievements? Is Morgan perhaps a poet's poet, as Elizabeth Bishop was in her lifetime, or the late Weldon Kees continues to be—a writer, that is, whose qualities speak strongly mostly to fellow practitioners of the art? Or, in Morgan's case, is something complex, singular, and elusive at work? The last hypothesis, I suggest, is closest to the truth. There is something unusual in Morgan's poetry that makes it difficult to understand, given conventional critical categories, and these intrinsic qualities are compounded by certain extrinsic issues that have made it doubly difficult for critics to assess his particular achievements as a poet.

There are at least three obvious reasons for the delay in Morgan's work achieving a proper estimation. The first has already been mentioned, namely the difficulty in American intellectual and artistic life of gaining prominence in a second field after one is already well-established in the first. Ambidexterity is not prized in our cultural life, which thrives on specialization, and versatility is often unjustly dismissed by specialists as amateurism. A career like T.S. Eliot's, with its almost equal distinction in poetry, criticism, editing, and drama, seems inconceivable in contemporary letters. The overestimation of specialized accomplishment reflects the influence of academic culture, and it often leads to odd distortions in critical reputations, especially those of writers outside the university where the pragmatic versatility of both public intellectuals and literary bohemians still necessarily prevails. Contemporary critics don't merely underestimate the wide-ranging careers of writers distinguished in multiple genres, they seem honestly baffled by them. Multi-talented writers like Howard Nemerov, Fred Chappell, or Weldon Kees seem genteelly punished rather than generously rewarded for their ambition. The implications of much criticism is that such promiscuous creativity seems unserious, unfocused, and indeed, almost improper. Despite the examples of Samuel Johnson,

Oliver Goldsmith, William Blake, Dante Gabriel Rossetti, Ralph Waldo Emerson, Edgar Allan Poe, Thomas Hardy, Rudyard Kipling, or D.H. Lawrence in English (not to mention the signal achievements of Goethe, Hugo, Pushkin, or Michelangelo in European literature), the assumption seems to be that serious artistic endeavor demands artistic specialization. Consequently we underestimate W.H. Auden's criticism, Robinson Jeffers's drama, Vladimir Nabokov's poetry, and Frederick Morgan's poetry.

The second extrinsic impediment to assessing Morgan as a poet comes from his extraordinarily late development as a writer — both in absolute terms and in comparison to his long-standing editorial career. By the age of thirty, Morgan was a notable editor; by forty he was a famous one. In contrast, he did not publish his first book of poems, which was significantly titled *A Book of Change* (1972), until he was fifty years old (and *The Hudson Review* was almost half that age). Despite our cult of youth, important American poets often delay their debut volumes until middle age. Robert Frost was thirty-nine when *A Boy's Will* (1913) appeared. Wallace Stevens was forty-three when *Harmonium* (1923) came out. William Stafford was forty-six at the time of his first book, *West of Your City* (1960), and there are many other examples. But these were inevitably poets who had written and published for years before bringing out a volume. After all, "A book of poems," as Wallace Stevens remarked, "is a damned serious thing."

Although Morgan had published a few poems in his early youth, he had essentially stopped writing verse by his mid-twenties after returning from his military service in World War II. He only began writing again a few years before *A Book of Change* — a gap of one quarter-century. In public perception his literary personality was already well formed by the time he emerged as a poet. But in a deeper sense there is something quite singular about a poet who emerges so late in life — well after youth, and well beyond even what Dante termed *nel mezzo del cammin di nostra vita*. The consequences of this late start are everywhere apparent in Morgan's poetic career — for both good and ill, this late start counts as one of the central facts of his poetic career.

On the negative side, *A Book of Change* is very much a beginner's volume — clear, heartfelt, well-shaped, but often under-realized. It is the work of a mature mind but not yet a mature poet. While the poems are never bad — Morgan's sensibility is too intelligent and well-governed for that—they are mostly not good enough. Much of the work in this thick, 160-page collection lacks resonance. But two things—to credit the positive side—are now obvious in retrospect. First, all of his later themes and concerns are already present in this debut volume. Second, the book demonstrates the stylistically diverse approach that would be the hallmark of his later work. *A Book of Change* contains everything from haiku-like short poems and triolets to prose poems and lyric sequences of unrhymed sonnets—a highly unusual approach for any book of that decade.

What no reader or critic could have predicted from *A Book of Change* —perhaps not even the poet himself—was the huge explosion of creativity that would follow over the next decade as Morgan made up for lost time. In order to understand that phenomenon, however, it is helpful to return to the oddity of his late development. There are two obvious questions to consider. Why did Morgan stop writing for twenty-five years? And why did he suddenly resume? As for the first question, in the absence of a biographical study, it is impossible for a critic to state conclusively the psychological or social forces that inhibited Morgan's poetic energy in the first part of his literary life (though common sense suggests that the rigors and displacement of military duty in World War II, the pressures of creating, building, and sustaining a major literary journal, and the responsibilities of raising a family of six children would not have aided poetic contemplation). But, if the sources of his long silence remain beyond accurate speculation, the causes of his poetic rejuvenescence seem indisputable. Two crucial events, one tragic, the other joyful, released Morgan's creative energies—the suicide of his son John in 1968 and his marriage to Paula Deitz in 1969. These events not only inform *A Book of Change*; they resonate through every subsequent volume. It is surely neither accidental nor insignificant that every book of poems Frederick Morgan has published from *A Book of Change* to the present volume, *The One Abiding* (2003), bear a similar dedication, namely "For Paula." Nor can any critic miss the obvious fact that Morgan's central poetic themes—early and late—have been love and death.

As noted earlier, Morgan's late beginnings as a poet were followed by an extraordinary explosion of creativity—a level of activity more typical of youthful frenzy than midlife deliberation. It would be fair to say that during the 1970s and early 1980s between the ages of fifty and sixty Frederick Morgan became one of the most interesting and ambitious young poets in America. In that remarkable decade, he published no less than four full-length collections of poetry, two smaller fine-press editions, a book of translations, and a superb book of prose parables. These books chronicled his rapid maturity and growing mastery of the art culminating in *Death Mother* (1979) and *Northbook* (1982), two of the finest collections published by any member of his generation. These books showed Morgan defining his personal voice, testing individual themes, and experimenting with various styles, displaying the energy and audaciousness that has characterized his work ever since. "One must shoot the works and not hold back," he remarked in a poem, and that statement might serve as a motto for his astonishing transformation into a poet of power, independence, and originality.

It is, however, precisely this originality that has represented the third impediment to Morgan's proper assessment. Just as *The Hudson Review* maintained its importance by remaining engaged but non-partisan in the political and ideological battles that dominate New York intellectual life, Morgan's poetry reveals a complete independence from the aesthetic and ideological conflicts that have typified American poetry over the past thirty years. His poetry has never chosen one approach to the exclusion of any other, nor positioned itself in one tradition to the exclusion of another. From the first, Morgan has written simultaneously in free and formal verse, in both impersonal and confessional modes, in narrative or lyric genres, in long and short works, in both verse and poetic prose. This situation renders most conventional critical approaches useless. Morgan simply cannot be placed by linking him reflexively to established writers. He belongs neither to the tribe of Wilbur nor Bly, Lowell nor Ginsberg, Sexton nor Merwin, Ashbery nor Ammons. He must be evaluated on his own terms — or not at all. This quality means that to describe his work a critic must build a definition from the poems themselves without recourse to the standard-issue ideologies of contemporary poetics. Under any circumstances, such studious assessment is a difficult and demanding task, but in a divisive and hyper-politicized literary age like ours, it appears almost impossible.

What then are the proper terms by which to discuss Morgan's work? What qualities seem intrinsic to his poetry? As a departure point, consider this eight-line poem from Morgan's 1977 volume, *Poems of the Two Worlds*.

THE STEP

From where you are at any moment you
may step off into death.
Is it not a clinching thought?
I do not mean a stoical bravado
of making the great decision blade in hand
but the awareness, all so simple, that
right in the middle of the day
you may be called to an adjoining room.

By contemporary literary standards, this provocative short poem is highly unusual. First, it is extremely brief, but not in the purely imagistic or aphoristic way that today's short poems tend to be. Second, it carries a clear, indeed unambiguous and paraphrasable message—namely the imminence of death in daily life. Third, the poem moves logically rather than associationally by stating and refining a single proposition that is offered simultaneously as an idea and an image.

"The Step," in fact, suggests something that might seem either naïve or even absurd to most poetry critics—namely that Morgan is more interested in what he is saying than in how he says it. Rather than style being the poem's central concern, instead it is the philosophy that the poem espouses. In this sense Morgan's poetry—with its starkly philosophical content and its unavoidable sense of spiritual urgency, curiously resembles another singular outsider in American poetry, Stephen Crane, whose compressed and imagistic existential parables seem equally rooted in real philosophical conviction.

Stark and compressed, "The Step" offers the advantage of presenting Morgan's work with an almost abstract clarity. But usually his poems move with slow and elegant elaboration. Listen to the mysterious delicacy of "Three Children Looking over the Edge of the World" from the 1979 volume *Death Mother and Other Poems*:

They came to the end of the road
and there was a wall across it
of cut stone—not very high.

Two of them boosted the third up
between them, he scrambled to the top
and found it wide enough to sit on easily.
Then he leaned back and gave the others a hand.

One two three in a row they sat there
staring: there was no bottom.
Below them a cliff went down and down for ever

and across from them, facing them, was nothing—
an emptiness that had no other side
and turned their vision back upon itself.

So there wasn't much to do or look at, after all.
One of them told a rhyme, the others chimed in,
and after a little while they swung around
and let themselves back down.

But when their feet touched solid road again
they saw at once they had dropped from the top of the sky
through sun and air and clouds and trees
and that the world was the wall.

In a philosophical sense, this poem articulates an almost identical worldview to "The Step," but, as a poem, its preoccupations and effects are entirely different—just as its relaxed but concise style marks a departure from the austere minimalism of the earlier poem. "Three Children Looking over the Edge of the World" is a gently allegorical lyric, a poetic coming-of-age parable about first glimpsing oblivion and death and how that primal insight changes everything in one's worldview. Once the children climb down from the wall after viewing nothingness, the entire cosmos is different.

Before trying to offer a preliminary description of Morgan's poetic sensibility, let me quote one more poem—which is both similar and distinct from the other two. Here is the fourth section of "The River," a sequence of short love poems written in 1980 (and dedicated, of course, "For Paula").

Now you are holding a book:
intelligence there with passion
surviving the individual brain and hand—

and when you speak of it tellingly
as we walk beneath the trees
        a living ghost stirs
in the world where all our thoughts are trees and rivers.

In some essential sense the worldview reflected in this short love poem is identical to that of the other two poems. Twice in this brief, seven-line poem the speaker alludes to our mortality—noting that the book his lover holds contains both intelligence and passion that survived the individual brain and hand that created it, and later in the paradoxical image of the living ghost. In other words, it survived the death of its author. But here those *memento mori* are refracted by the lyrical joy of being alive and being loved in the physical world, and expressed in an intimate style slightly reminiscent of Chinese or Japanese lyric poetry.

To use these three poems as a starting point to develop a description of Morgan's work already suggests certain difficulties in definition. Although all published in a four-year period (between 1977 and 1980), the poems exhibit astonishing differences—at least in formal terms. They show three distinct styles, three differing tones, and three separate points of view, linked only by a common worldview or philosophy. A reader might initially believe that Morgan considered poetry primarily a philosophical vehicle and had little interest in language *per se* as a poetic medium. For reasons that will be explained in a moment, that is a superficial and mistaken assumption, but this misapprehension has probably clouded some discussions of his work. In our period, poetry has so often announced its aims and allegiances through style, sensibility, and form that it is difficult for many readers to conceive of other qualities informing and unifying a body of work.

Any ambitious poet faces a serious challenge in trying to expand his or her imaginative concerns without compromising the creative authenticity or individual sensibility of the work. How does a poet—in other words—grow honestly into new modes of expression, new forms, new styles, new genres, and new subjects? How does the writer change—or at the very least—expand without losing the genuine creative impetus that inspired the earlier poems? There is always the very real danger of faking inspiration or borrowing the modes and manners of other writers.

This dilemma is surely heightened in Morgan's case by his quite sensible belief that inspiration is involuntary. "The poem comes as a gift," he has remarked, "I can only see it that way. . . you can't force a poem." Morgan has solved this challenge—perhaps unconsciously—by cultivating at least three different points of view in his poetry, all of them personal, if not always autobiographical. If Frederick Morgan has had two public lives (as editor and poet), he has also led three poetical lives in his work. He has cultivated side by side in his work, from his first book to the present, three versions of himself—the child, the lover, and the philosopher.

All three personalities reflect a certain point of view, all philosophically consistent but poetically diverse. The child in Morgan's poetry greets the world initially in joy and wonder but inevitably gets a glimpse of the terror of extinction. These contemporary poems of innocence are often autobiographical, as in "The Turtle" or "Washington Square." But they are just as often impersonal, even mythic, as in "The Ghost" or "Captain Blaze," where the protagonist is not a child, but the sensibility comes from the horror or adventure stories of childhood. (Morgan has more than once listed the pulp journal *Weird Tales* as a decisive early literary passion.) Morgan's encyclopedic interest in mythology, including Norse, Greek, Hindu, Jewish, and Buddhist lore, is surely one distinctive feature of his work. His characteristic treatment of mythology almost inevitably reveals that youthful sense of awe and pleasure in the characters and stories, especially violent stories, so often found in boyhood books of myths and legends. That fascination with violence and violent ends is not tangential because Morgan's most recurring, indeed most obsessive, theme is death. His child's perspective is simply the most distant and detached observer of human vulnerability and mortality.

The second perspective is the lover—a person closer to death because he is older but also one farther from death because he has found life's greatest consolation. There is no assurance of the afterlife in Morgan's worldview. His religious vision is closer to Buddhism than Christianity. Whatever consolation one secures, therefore, is achieved here and now with personal extinction always in the background. This perspective, of course, is not unusual for lyric poetry. It is the same insight found in Horace's *carpe diem* ode from two thousand years ago and all its myriad descendants. It is no surprise, then, that Morgan, whose poetic character is so nobly stoic in the Roman manner, would develop the Latin lyric tradition in his love poetry. Andrew Marvell's famous formulation, "The grave's a fine and private place / But none I think do there embrace," might well also serve as the motto of Morgan's amatory verse.

Certainly one of Morgan's central enterprises has been the reinvention of the contemporary love poem. No other major poet of his generation has written so many direct and (to appropriate a delicious word from the current academic lexicon) unproblematicized love lyrics. In his recent collection, *Poems for Paula* (1995), Morgan even arranged those poems not overtly about love in such a way that they served as philosophical commentaries on the love poems around them. In Morgan's *oeuvre*, love is not a youthful distraction or sensory escape; it is the summit (with art itself) of human aspiration, and to express and commemorate love in poetry represents for him a great human gesture. Love is, to borrow phrasing from one of Morgan's poems:

. . . a place of high vantage from which,

as from a mountain meadow,
future and past recede, and
the road itself lose[s] its meaning. . . .

His definition of love implicitly restates the traditional aims of religious mysticism in secular experiential terms. The mention of mysticism and its longing to escape the prison of temporal existence suggests Morgan's third poetic life—the philosopher.

In terms of age, Morgan's philosopher is the oldest of his three poetic incarnations. The philosophical persona seen so vividly in poems like his powerful sequences "Death Mother" and "Orpheus to Eurydice" or his great lyrics, "The Summit" and "February 11, 1977," is a man who has known love—both erotic and familial. He is also a man who has seen war, destruction, disease, and age. He knows—indeed physically feels—the imminent and unavoidable presence of death. Few contemporary poets have ever conveyed the horror of that realization more vividly than Morgan. (Just try to read "Death Mother" without flinching.) Fewer still have reached the liberating joy beyond that existential and physical horror that emerges in Morgan's finest philosophical poems.

However rooted in its own stoic perspective, Morgan's philosopher is never a man who denies the wonder and delight of the child or the comfort and ecstasy of the lover. It is precisely the imaginative ability to create those three personae or life stages in his work, and to explore their distinct qualities without losing the subtle harmonies of their co-existence, that is Morgan's artistic triumph. Publishing his first book at fifty, and reaching poetic maturity as he approached sixty, he found the poetic means to recapitulate his life experience in his work, without ever sacrificing the hard-won wisdom of his age. John Keats once famously praised a poet's "negative capability" to extinguish his own personality and become someone else. Frederick Morgan deserves praise for his positive capability—his power not to extinguish himself but to rediscover and reanimate each stage of his life in his poetry. This positive capability allows him to summon the child, the lover, and the philosopher, each to tell his story or perform his song.

There is more to be said about Morgan's poetry—his distinctive and pervasive use of mythology from the classical Greek and Roman to the unusual Norse and Hindu; his masterful mixture of Western and Eastern poetic technique (that intermingles American, European, Chinese, and Japanese styles); his bold reinvention of the supernatural narrative poem (that combines the tradition of Coleridge and Keats with those of H.P. Lovecraft and Sheridan LeFanu); his austere and steady religious vision (that begins in Mediterranean Stoicism but rises to Eastern transcendentalism). But one must leave something for future critics. Although Morgan's work stands outside the conventional explanations of contemporary American poetry, it is sufficiently strong and enduring that those explanations will need to be reformulated to account for his accomplishments.

It seems appropriate to end on the humane and enlarging notion of positive capability. Morgan's particular power has been to summon three voices to articulate one philosophy, to transcend time in a mysteriously Trinitarian feat of imagination, to cultivate self-extinction in the service of self-discovery. So that by assuming three lives, he vividly expresses one complete life. One can't help reflecting that his remarkable poetic ability to escape the pressures and particulars of the self in its present moment and condition is also part of the same genius that made Morgan a truly great editor, one who could recognize, develop, and refine the strong and even unruly talents of other writers. So, it appears, my entire line of argument has been mistaken. There are not three Frederick Morgans, or even two. There is only one uniquely gifted, indomitably imaginative, and inimitable man whose life work has enhanced and enlarged our literature.

When the soul begins again to mount, it comes not to something alien but to its very self . . .

PLOTINUS

I

WASHINGTON SQUARE

Late in the twenties when I was small
in breezy spring and sullen fall
I walked each day to Washington Square
to play with other children there:
  Paul, the minister's son,
  Laura, who loved to run,
Benjamin with his costly toys,
and Sue, who said she hated boys.

Near the north entrance to the park
we'd meet at noon and play till dark
wide-ranging through those endless hours
as though all time and space were ours —
  for when we five combined
  we paid the hours no mind
so dazzled were we by the maze
of wonders opening to our gaze.

Each day that passed revealed a world —
a landscape secretly unfurled
to our five pairs of eyes alone.
As king or queen each ruled his own
  in turn, day after day,
  in strict sequence and sway,
and fixed its boundaries and decreed
the laws which all the rest must heed.

For justice governed all our play:
no single passion might outweigh
the claims of all to equal share
in treasure unforeseen and rare.
  And so we roamed at ease
  through joyful seigneuries

each vassal proven by the sword
loyal to Lady or to Lord.

I still recall those ancient games! —
the talismans, the secret names,
the questing knights and demoiselles
the wizards weaving crafty spells,
     and best of all our fair
     strong fortress-castle, where
tired and exultant, friend by friend,
we met at each adventure's end.

So the weeks passed—until one day
when I arrived at noon to play
near the great Arch, at the usual place,
I found no welcoming form or face:
     no comrade had appeared.
     I waited, watched and feared—
then wandered, aimlessly alone,
up and down those paths of stone.

This was a world, it seemed, this bare
immensity where here and there
dim random shapes loomed into view—
this was the world that strangers knew.
     I, its frailest part,
     received it from the start
as closer to the quick of things
than all our brave imaginings.

I stared straight up at the pale sky
where hulks of cloud went drifting by
and knew myself alone and pure.
"Whatever comes, you shall endure,"
     a voice spoke inwardly,
     a voice not strange to me.

I tracked my hand across my face
and felt the world shift in its place.

Next day all seemed restored. My four
good friends returned—we roamed once more,
releasing brighter energies
as though we'd found new selves to please.
        Thus other months sped by
        and seasons changed, as I,
aware that all must pass away,
lived on intensely day to day.

Comrades!—how has life served you all?
Benjy grew up a drunkard, Paul
was killed in Normandy, and Sue
moved somewhere west, was lost from view.
        Sweet Laura, first to go,
        died of the polio
in '33—my love, aged ten.
Sometimes I wish you back again,

the four of you, just as you were,
triumphant in that eager stir
of childhood—and myself with you
as I was then . . . But it won't do.
        No dream of holding fast
        to a beloved past
can cloud the heads of those who know
what's dead is dead, and rightly so.

Children still play in Washington Square
but they don't roam free, they must beware—
gone is their ancient liberty.
Gone, too, that civic decency
        which cherished old and young
        who shared the common tongue.

America bows to new, weak gods;
its children play against the odds.

Laura, Benjamin, Paul and Sue,
you've gone your ways. I'm going, too.
Our early joys were dearly bought —
the world was never what we thought —
    and yet, we're justified:
    it wasn't we who lied.
Now leave me, friends, and leaving, bless.
Once more I face the emptiness.

ELEVENTH STREET

Waking at first light in my third-floor room,
I'd wait in bed for morning's earliest sounds:
a cough, a random call, the scraping broom
of the sidewalk sweeper starting on his rounds—

then brightly clear at last from the waking street
the milk-man's horse clop-clopping down from Fifth,
the milk-man's "Whoa!" when he paused at our kitchen gate,
and the big cans clanking softly in his grip

as he went down the steps to our cook's "Good morning, Pete."
"Good morning, Lizzie, you're prettier every day—"
and a moment later he'd hoist himself back on his seat,
give a loud "Geeup!" and they'd clop-clop on their way—

and I'd stretch myself and yawn and scramble from bed
thinking of the endless day that lay ahead.

FROM THE GUEST ROOM WINDOW

A gray autumn day.
Down in our back yard
green shrubs are washed by rain.

At the far end
the little naked boy
stands patiently holding his dolphin.
His basin is empty.
The fountain has been turned off for the winter.

A few leaves litter the pathways of paved stone.

All is still.
Now, suddenly, a gust of rain—
the green shrubs twist in the wind.

At left a gray cat creeps along the fence-top.
It leaps into our neighbors' yard and quickly disappears.

THE REFUGE

High in his small neat bedroom
he wove his fantasy tales
of magic aspiration—
refuges from the real

which he'd been taught to fear
as a thing one mustn't trust
and thus had little purchase on
(he'd live to count the cost).

Raised on books and solitude,
knowing only himself,
he'd nonetheless caught glimpses of
a vast surrounding life

that horrified and tempted. How
could he learn its wrongs and rights?
Safer, he thought, to linger on
within the enchanted gates

than venture three flights down and out
into that dubious realm
where strangers knowing what he did not
might try him and condemn.

And so he'd watch there, wondering
until his mother returned
from shopping, fresh and loving,
not knowing how he'd yearned.

THE CHRISTMAS TREE

In the quiet house, on a morning of snow,
the child stares at the Christmas Tree.
He wonders what there is to know

behind the tinsel and the glow—
behind what he's been taught to see
in the quiet house, on mornings of snow,

when he's snug indoors with nowhere to go
and mother and father have let him be:
he wonders if there's more to know

about their bright, triumphant show
than he's been told. Is the brave Tree,
so proud in the house on this morning of snow,

all that it seems? He gathers no
assurance from its silent glee
and fears there must be more to know

than one poor child can learn. If so
what stake may he claim in the mystery?
He stares from the house at the falling snow
and wonders how he'll ever know.

THE CLOCK

The boy had an odd dream on Christmas Eve.
He went floating through the night in the old hall clock,
now changed into a boat. The moon was up.
A being like himself sat at his side.

His house left far behind, the objects in it
took on with distance strange lives of their own,
secretive and severe. He sensed them there,
holding among themselves dark conversation.

Now there were fields below him, cloaked in white,
with here and there a barn or naked tree.
In burrows deep beneath the snow, he knew,
the speechless animals were warmly bundled.

His double waved a hand, and all at once
the sun blazed out full strength and the world was changed!
A tropic greenness overspread the land,
dotted with fruit trees and bright-blooming flowers.

Behind the beauty, though, a malice lurked—
a hint, it seemed to him, of something shrouded,
not yet revealed, but charged with pain and loss.
Seized with a sudden grief he cried out loud

and saw his semblance shrivel into smoke
as the clock rolled over, dropping him down down
through alternations of the moon and sun
to a place of shadows and ambiguous voices . . .

He woke in his narrow bed to a rainy Christmas.

1932

At Twelfth Street and Fifth Avenue
in front of the old Longchamps
one frigid winter morning, as
I watched for the bus to come,

I saw a dark unshaven man
whose skin was snowy pale
set up a stand at the corner. He
had bright red apples for sale

a nickel each, but no one stopped
to look: they walked on by.
He stood there coatless, shivering,
with a fever in his eye

until a small blond shape appeared,
a child of three or four,
who came from nowhere I could see—
no one accompanied her.

She wore a blue wool coat, fur-trimmed
to warm her wrists and neck,
fur hat, thick gloves and leggings to block
the cold from every crack—

she ran straight to the tattered man,
hugged him around both knees,
tipped back her head and stared straight up:
I couldn't read her gaze.

And there they stood, she holding fast
as though she'd seized her own,

he making no move to escape
but smiling grimly down . . .

I never saw the end, nor learned
what it was those two might tell.
My bus pulled up, I climbed aboard—
and was on my way to school.

II

MAY NIGHT

By midnight all the street noises were stilled
except for now and then a slamming door,
a gust of muffled laughter, or—in the distance—
the old Sixth Avenue El's receding roar.

You stood at the window. I had left off playing
Schumann's *Des Abends* on the scratched upright
and turned to you now, thinking at last you'd utter
such words as had eluded us all night.

Your gaze gave back my own. Your pensive eyes,
aglint with tears, darkened as though to warn me
that even now our great game might be lost,

and so I rose, not speaking, and stood by you—
and saw then, on your desk in the dim corner,
that opened letter, vengeful as a ghost.

DOLORES

After the night of pain
you did your vanishing act,
Dolores—I didn't see you again
through all that winter of war.

Those "white and heavy limbs"
on which my own would rest
after our lust had run its course
withdrew into the chill

of far New England towns
from which as winter waned
you sent your fitful messages,
obscure and menacing.

"There'll never be an end!"
"I need the pain you bring me."
"I'll come to you once more, and kneel—
and you'll be mine for ever."

Black ink on pale mauve paper—
your bold and spidery hand . . .
the words cut deep as they were meant,
they left a bitter yearning,

yet I withheld reply
and let the pain absorb
trusting that when those wounds had healed
I'd still be unforgiving.

You weren't quite divine,
you see, for all your beauty,

for all that marbled reticence
masking the inner fires—

not yet a perfect idol
despite your cold eyelids
and brazen cruelty of gaze—
no, I could not concede it,

but glimpsed you in my dreams
as a frail puppet-thing
with eyes like dead-bright moons, stumbling
alone down endless vistas . . .

And so when next we met,
one mild midsummer night,
I kissed you once and set you free
in that new wilderness.

SEPTEMBER 1957

White sky in the last light.
      Imminence of trees.
Pale birch-clumps amid gray trunks of pine.

Black branchings on the white
      remoteness. Tracework.
Visible clusterings, division of leaves.

Pale page of emptiness
      on which some hand had scribbled
a message in impenetrable code—

for years he pondered it:
      how to retrieve it,
how to redeem that last hope and despair.

GIFTS

The gift he once ventured
in weak generosity
was offered too soon
yet too late to be withdrawn.

The woman, serene
in her unhindered progress,
had been blessed long before
though not by this man.

Prime and unsharable
that earliest gift,
that lasting exemption
from day-to-day anguish—

as though she were an Eve
to whom the Lord had spoken:
"Go free—I love thy waywardness.
The pain shall be his."

"YOU STIRRED SO GENTLY
ON THE BED . . ."

You stirred so gently on the bed
it was as though you hadn't moved
except as one small wavelet moves
    in the receding tide.

Was it a dream enticing you
with hint of horrors unforeseen?
Briefly, I glimpsed a savage gleam
    in your half-opened eyes.

The tide had ebbed and left you there,
woman I'd known for many a year—
but who was I to call you back
    from the dream that never died?

THE RECREANT

Voices at evening over the water
echoing or remembered
brought him word of one abiding . . .

Abiding, yes — and unforgiving?
Not yet, he hoped, on this pale evening
washed by damp breezes from the bay —
the tide receding.

What was it that had tempted him
to wander from her pathways?
Glimmer of some false dawn, perhaps,
burning beyond the waves?
The memories, the echoings returned —
all pain and waste for lack of one abiding.

Wasted. Night after night he felt
an insurmountable grief
in all those couplings with soft teasing bodies

as hour by hour her cool voice murmured, "Careful . . .
In the end, you know, I turn my other face."

THE PARTING

I stood in the pine wood waiting for my friend
by the path along the water—
night falling, one last lobster boat
throbbing in from the bay.
I wished to say farewell, *bonne chance*!
I did not expect to see this man again.

"It's the end, I guess," he said, "but first
I'm glad we can share such a moment.
You've loved this place for years, quite as much as I,
and must surely know what I'm feeling
now that my time has come to leave it behind.
What a heart-breaking sunset! Yes, I'm glad you're with me . . .

Still, you'll agree, I haven't been lucky here,
and maybe this moving on will help me find
whatever it is I've wanted.
I feel like being alone high up in the mountains—
the Rockies, maybe, or Tibet:
I might come upon something like truth—and if I die, so be it."

We watched the swollen sun sink redly seaward
and stood for a time not speaking—then shook hands.
"Goodbye," I said. "Prevail.
May life serve you well while it lasts!
I know you and I will be called as one, in the end."
He smiled . . . I pulled from my hip the flask of brandy
and we each took a sip before he turned and went.

III

ANAKTORIA

Now that you have made your great renunciation
do you think of us, in our cold city,
those many of us who loved you,
those who have held you close—
do you remember our faces, the touch of our hands and lips?

Something about you had been secured from death,
or so we felt
(fresh, perhaps, from your strong embrace)—
and to watch you while all thoughtlessly you danced
was to share a fierce joy we couldn't quite comprehend.

Now, you move beneath a desert sky
among foreigners, are touched by other hands—
but at night, when the moon rises coldly above our avenues,
we recall old days of triumph
and see you again in our midst:
lean body, candid profile, glittering hair.

"I CALLED UP MYRTIS FROM
THE DEAD..."

I called up Myrtis from the dead
to be my friend and lover.
She placed both hands upon my head
and burned me with a fever,

saying, "Strange man, how can you hope
to make your peace with evil days,
with vermin who infest your land
and soil the beauty of its ways?

Withdraw, and leave them to their filth.
Their illness is not yours to cure
who've drawn your strength from ancient things
and healed your own despair.

Withdraw into the secret life!"
Gently she touched my face—
then faded, leaving me to mourn
and call up Talos in her place.

ACTAEON

Actaeon, changed to stag, was ripped
by jaws of ignorant hounds
for having spied the unmentionable
while wandering out of bounds.

And yet, he sinned in innocence
not knowing she was near:
her land had not been posted,
its boundaries were unclear.

It takes a deity, you'll say,
to be so cruel, so unfair!
Too true—but that's the way it works.
At least, he'd seen that Body, bare.

PASIPHAË

When fair Pasiphaë craved the bull
    she took heroic measures —
engaged the famed artificer
    to guarantee her pleasures.

He built a comely cow of wood
    covered in soft cow-hide,
politely showed the queen how best
    to arrange herself inside,

and left her in a fragrant field
    where the bull would often roam.
It came, and with a bull's finesse
    soon made itself at home.

The outcome was an unlikely lad
    half brute, half man, they say —
a tortuous labyrinth was built
    to keep him stashed away —

but proud Pasiphaë had her wish
    and ruled for many a year
praising the mighty Ocean Lord
    who'd charmed away her fear.

HYPATIA

εἰς οὐρανὸν γάρ ἐστι σοῦ τὰ πράγματα

When the vile monks of Nitria
butchered the chaste philosopher
their new God triumphed, so it seemed:
the old ones had forsaken her.

This murder took place years ago,
in March, anno domini 415,
during the holy time of Lent.
Alexandria was the scene.

Hypatia the neoplatonist,
while driving to her school to teach,
was cornered by the filthy swarm
who cursed her for a pagan bitch

and pulled her from her chariot.
The woman was without defense:
she'd scorned the warnings of her friends,
relying on her innocence.

They dragged her to the nearest church
(it seemed the most appropriate place)
and stripped her naked there, and jeered,
howling with glee at her disgrace —

then beat her down to the sacred floor
and hacked the live flesh from her bones
with tiles and shards and oyster shells —
then hoisted high the sad remains

and marched in triumph up and down
the city's colonnaded ways,

shouting the praises of their God
and vengeance on his enemies.

They burned all that was left of her—
last of the great Plotinian line,
Theon's daughter, Synesius' friend,
humbled to dust by Coptic swine.

The bishop who had egged them on,
Cyril (later canonized),
made known to all the outside world
he was displeased, shocked, mortified

by this excess of righteous zeal.
Still, he kept safe his scurvy crew
by bribing all the magistrates:
he'd have more work for them to do . . .

And that was it. Hypatia died.
The old gods faded past recall.
A new god triumphed—if new he was,
and not the oldest one of all.

IN THE PRIVATE HOSPITAL

At the first touch of dawn I heard the horn-calls, golden and muted,
    far in the distance. They must come, I knew, from the forest—
    from somewhere within that shaded immensity which was
    visible just outside my window

(for I seemed to be lodged at the heart of it) verdant and rustling, and
    extending perhaps for hundreds of miles. Who or what was
    being hunted, I wondered,

and who were the pursuers? The sound drew nearer, then was cut off
    abruptly—and I seemed to hear, from the middle distance, faint
    cries whose sense I could not grasp.

Broad awake, I trembled in my bed—between those cool soft sheets
    whose touch had grown familiar during my long convalescence.
    I shook uncontrollably without knowing why,

for was I not secure here, had I not been saved from burning? I was
    whole again and free of pain: surely someone must wish me
    well. I searched my mind for clues to this miraculous healing,

but found I could remember nothing since the night of dread, when I'd
    been torched and left for dead in the old burning city.

—How many weeks or months had passed, and how had I been
    rescued? Those strong hands that had tended me—to whom did
    they belong, what was their motive?

Was the truth by any chance that I had died? Had I donned a new life
    in this altered world? As the day grew silently bright

I could make out, as though seeing them for the first time, the details
    of my neat, airy room: off at my right the white closed door

(through which, I now remembered, a nurse came and went),
and along the wall facing me

the few simple articles of furniture—a desk and chair, a table, a small
dresser—all of them polished and new and made of natural
wood—

wood, I could tell, that held the beauty and variety of the forest in its
grain; wood that had been worked by people who understood it—

and near me at my left the window, opening to leafy vastness and
framed by trim white curtains swaying gently in the morning
breeze.

All at once I took heart. "This bliss is real," I thought, "I must retain
it. Whatever my story may prove to be, I must not lose this."
Again a horn sounded,

and in terror I remembered the dream: how at darkest hour of night
my Nurse had come to me and passed her skilled hands up and
down my body,

making me groan in ecstasy and fear. I spent myself, she caressed me.
"Soon you will be well," she had whispered. "Soon you will be
quite ready."

THE TOWER

From the grey tower in his dream
a chime tolled through the night
putting the maddened birds to flight—

those birds that strayed beyond the dream
into our restless day
and sought the terminus of death,
but never found their way.

IV

THE SIGN

We came to a low bare hill
and climbed its rocky side,
and found where right at the top
someone had been crucified.

The cross was made of cedar,
its foot wedged deep between stones,
and it canted forward gently
to show off its load of bones.

A short but stocky skeleton
was bound to the unyielding wood
by chains so tightly clenched
they'd hold it there for good—

or so at least it seemed,
for the bones were mostly in place.
I took a step or two forward
to look the thing in its face.

"A short man but a bruiser,"
said Schwartz, after he and Hall
and I had made our inspection.
But was it a man at all?

The rib-cage was intact—
the pelvic structure, too—
the spine had held its place
though ever so slightly skewed,

and the skull remained entire
with lower jaw still hinged.

We all three stared and stared at it,
and it stared right back and grinned.

If this was a man, he'd been fashioned
too bulky and thick for his height,
with a head unpleasantly large
and proportions that hadn't come right.

Yes, it looked like a man—but was hateful.
That much came clear to my mind
as I fought off obscure intimations
of something still worse near at hand . . .

"It's an odd kind of ape, I imagine,"
said Hall, "though I'm really not sure,
or maybe a freak, or mutant,
a being that filled them with fear

and blind horror, the people who did this—
who left him to parch and starve
and suffer such ultimate torment.
One wonders what people they were."

"And why on a cross?" muttered Schwartz.
"Did it matter so much how he died?
Was blasphemy what they were after?
And where does the evil reside—

in this hideous sacrificed thing
(and to me it looks evil as sin)
or in those who condemned him?" Well, clearly
Hall and I had no answer for him,

so I only asked, "What to do now?"
"Nothing," said Hall. "Let him be.
Were you thinking of Christian burial!"
Schwartz groaned—and said, "I agree."

It was settled. We'd never reveal it,
this secret so grand and malign.
We descended, resuming our journey,
and left him up there as a Sign.

THE BURIAL

How shall the difficult man
be buried? How indeed?
Who can track the difficult man
or know where he keeps himself hid?

You must catch him first if you can,
making certain he's safe in his box,
then put the whole works in that other—
the one with permanent locks.

Having settled him down once for all
in an absence that's yours to command
you may streamline his speech into scripture
and take all his meanings in hand—

you may smooth out the sense of his riddles
that taxed the dull wits of the tribe,
assign him a throne up in heaven
and yelp the good news far and wide—

but it's useless. Eluding your grasp,
he goes drifting away through the mist
as you stand there clutching the castoffs
from which he implausibly slipped—

and what have you gained for your trouble?
No enlightenment, no guarantee:
just this box which will rot in that other
while the difficult man roams free.

THE RETURN

I waited there, outside of Time,
until my time should come.
You didn't think about me much—
it was enough for you to clutch
those brighter trophies you had won.

But now I'm here in my full being—
naked, brutish, plain as day.
What can you say to those you love
except, there's one you more than love
who must now have her way?

THE FRIEND

I think of you this winter noon
sun glinting from our icy streets
and wonder at life's chances, how
each day renews the pangs of loss

for those like you who, year by year,
while others fawned and bent the knee,
held to a difficult true course,
learning too late the rules had changed.

You lost it all—but still endure
in some strange latitude of time
walking a seacoast strewn with wrecks
unpitied and unpitying,

and if you signal me, it's from
a past perhaps that never was
wherein you're gloriously at home
foretelling our bold destinies—

foretelling, too, another life,
the one that never came about,
in which you gaily won it all
and never learned to fear or doubt.

THE SHAMROCK

"I've great days then godawful ones —
I'm in heaven, then deep in the pits —
I try to take them all in stride
without losing my wits

but just can't get the hang of it!"
That's what Tim said one night
in the Shamrock Grill off Lexington.
The bottles were burning bright,

the juke-box aglow as the Clancy Brothers
belted out "Finnegans Wake"
and I stood at the bar drinking Bushmill's
with Timmy for old times' sake.

"Confucius said that at seventy
he'd 'achieved an unperturbed mind.'
Me now, I'm only sixty-six —
do you think I might still have time?"

It was there at the bar three months later
I had word that Tim was dead,
and downed a last glass in his honor
before walking home to bed.

THE BODY

The body frozen in the lake
      rose up again in spring.
It could not be identified
at first, despite the golden hair,
      despite the ruby ring.

Its finder could not shake the chill
      and suffered sleepless nights
while law and medicine assumed
their harsh assignments, and the press
      performed its squalid rites.

It was the teeth that told the tale:
      a woman from away
who'd said goodbye to the warm Gulf
and placid coasts of pine and scrub
      one bright midsummer day,

and driven north a thousand miles
      to the city on the lake.
Then came six changes of address,
smart clothes, chic night-clubs, and new friends
      whose names could not be traced.

The owner of a roadside inn
      where she and a man had stayed
remembered that long yellow hair
and how she had "the sweetest smile,"
      but sometimes seemed afraid—

and other fragments of her past
      came drifting into view . . .
The finder of the body, though,

felt such strange harrowing within
        he could not see it through,

but left the city on the lake
        before the cold returned.
For twenty years the memory
of that poor body, rising up,
        lurked in his heart and burned,

until she came to him in dream
        with flowers in her hands
and said, "Forget me, patient friend,
for where I am love has its end,
        and *no one* understands."

RECOLLECTIONS OF JAPAN

1

The garden in the hills
shadowy still at dawn
shows no trace of footprints.
And yet, spring has arrived:
the snow is melting patchily.

2

Wild blossoms on the river banks
sway yellow in the rising wind:
see—their images bloom too,
deep in the watery clarities.

3

Warm light floods the countryside.
Summer is all about
and the green takes on a different tone
a shade or two beyond
the green that was here before.

4

A hasty rendez-vous
on the lonely mountain meadow—
our pillows are of grass:
nor shall we ever speak one word
of this our dew-drenched meeting.

5

How long will it endure?
My dear, I cannot tell.
I do not know your heart—
only the intricate tangles of
this dark rich-flowing hair.

6

No moon in the sky tonight.
Is this cold autumn the same
as autumns now gone by?
Though I myself remain,
am I the I I was?

7

What am I then to do
when the harsh winds blow through
this withered trellis?
The leaves are turning brown,
I have nowhere to hide.

8

Through rifts in the night clouds
adrift in winter winds
shafts of bright moonlight pierce
shining remote and cold.

9

And the ruthless winds still blow
at midnight as I wonder—

would I have been thus lonely
home in my own great city?

10

A long year has passed
but this is not what I had hoped for.
The parched fields of summer are
far less arid than
these letters from a withered friend.

MEDITATION AT SUNDOWN

In memory of my son Seth

I

It takes me aback at times,
this slow disease for which
I no longer have a name.

Old names are out of fashion
and the new ones unconvincing:
one suffers nonetheless.

What cure? In the search itself?
In the striving? Don't believe it,
but give the beast his due.

2

From the being born to the dying
life is a butchery.
The primitives got it right
with their ritual compensations.

For those more enlightened, however,
the unacceptable lurks
just beyond the visible circle—
knife at the ready.

3

People dressed in the styles
of the 1880s and '90s
visit me sometimes after dark.

They gaze about my rooms
in their graceful twos and threes
uncertain how to proceed.

They don't like what they see!
I feel it, though they're tactful and
unwilling to give offense.

"Be of good cheer," I tell them.
"Soon I'll be one of you,
stuffless and serene —

all beauties and contingencies
having drifted safely down
to the place of timeless patchwork."

4

You bear the mark of what you are
as children bear the marks of their abusers.

You do not know just what it is you've done,
nor what was done to you.

Deep in your mind a scumbled mountain rises —
so huge, you'd swear it reaches to the sky!

You sleep, and see in dreams the bridge
on which you may not build.

Black water plays beneath. The span
is brief, the far shore dimmed in mist.

Before the great resumption,
a time of fitting anguish.

And the heart is stopped, almost,
in paroxysm of loss
outside the gates that may stay closed for good.

I think of the Chinese masters
in their shacks beneath the moon:
wine and chrysanthemums,
the dignities of exile.

V

THE WATCHER

I stand here at the crossroads
near the gray strip of beach
among these windblown pines.

Thoughts move through my mind
like clouds through a calm sky—
slower than life, unhurried.

I grant rest to the traveler:
he throws himself down at my feet
and sleeps his way through sorrow.

In grimmest dog-day heat
my ancient fount still brims
with cold unsullied water

while night by moonless night
these two eyes chill as stars
gleam out from the worn mask.

Question not what I am.
Solitary in this place
I lead strange lives elsewhere

and thus am reckoned god:
"god of the rocks and pines"
is how you might conceive it . . .

Worship me then, if you choose,
as one who dreams and waits.
The truth will follow after.

A DREAM

I found myself in James's Great Good Place
or Cambridge, perhaps, a hundred years ago:
long days of Spring, tall elms, unhurried youths,
huge halls of soft stone aging in the sun.
I tried to understand how I had come here.
Was this mild place my proper destination?
Was it a fraud? Or some odd stop-off point
along a further road I yet must travel?

In a great mess-hall underneath dim flags
I sat at table between you, my good friends:
you priestly at the head, expounding, smiling —
you at my right, extending gentle hands.
We solved the world's great Riddle then, so deftly
I knew when I awoke I'd neared the end.

THE PRIEST

Sacrificing
to the four quarters
I find the winds responsive.

The rains come
as the gods decree.
I give thanks and go barefoot, laughing.

How many lives have possessed me —
how many gods have I served?

I remember a parching summer
and a voice crying out from a thorn-bush:
it came from the broken skull
of a traveler long ago murdered
whose ghost remained tethered there, raging.
Oh the anger, the pain that consumed me
as our minds intertwined in the heat!

And I think of a year of great snow
when climbing the lavender mountain
I found halfway up a deep cave
in which seven black bears had sought shelter.
Seven — and I made the eighth,
who lingered and dozed one whole season
dreaming my life as a man.

Through how many lives have I traveled,
in how many shapes found my being?

Alert now, at ease
in each moment that blossoms and fades
I know myself common as clay
yet all the while kin to the gods,
at home with their vigors and skills.

When I dream, I am one with their dreaming:
their lives come to bear on my own
which long years ago was made ready,
swept clean for the great arrivals.

&

I was born on the northernmost island,
a woodcutter's only son —
spent my early years sweating and slaving
obedient to my father.

On the day of his death I left home,
went wandering alone through the forest:
learned strength, self-dominion from the black pine,
quietude from the night sky.

NOTHING

Nothing, and naked —
thus he confronted the day
mistrusting all motives
but sure of his way.

Released from the past,
he contained it within
as structure and bone
of the men he had been.

At ease in his choices,
knowing evil and good,
might he now bring to focus
what it was he understood?

For he understood *something*,
on his windy plateau,
that quickened his heart-beat
and made his eyes glow.

RAIN

Rain, all enduring rain
that afternoon in the country cemetery:
a dripping, placid rain,
a rain intending to stay.

Dull, quiet fields all about us.
A closed horizon.
Tricklings of rain on the gravestones,
the freshening smell of grass.

The dead were there beneath us—
who they had been didn't matter.
Future and past didn't matter,
nor even our own dear selves.

I kissed you on the lips then
(there were rain-drops on your forehead)
and you drew your body closer
as we made that moment ours.

"WHEN I AWOKE AT LAST..."

τὴν ἐναντίαν δὲ δραμοῦσα ἥξει
οὐκ εἰς ἄλλο, ἀλλ᾽ εἰς αὑτὴν

When I awoke at last from the desperate dream
a morning mist was drifting off the islands.
I looked down on an empty beach—
saw rocks, saw birds, saw clumps of weed
and the mild waves rolling in.
The song—could I still be hearing it?—still pierced me.

What else did I remember? Shapes of terror,
deep anguish, crazed pursuit.
I groaned, and strove to fight free of it all,
all but that song—voiceless, indeterminate—
which through the dream's long sway had been transcending it
and now, it seemed, survived.
It came, I thought, from a place between sleep and waking.

I rose up then from the grass where I'd been lying
and stretched, and walked about,
and found close by, where the sparse soil edged the rocks,
the ancient image of a threshold god.
He was faceless now and seemingly abandoned—
but I prayed to him nonetheless.

"God of these shores, experienced, enduring—
assayer of all wayward, transient things—
modest master of the moment's chances—
strengthen me, please, for onward voyaging."
As I spoke the words a huge sleep overcame me,
and I dropped to the ground where I stood, and closed my eyes.

Hours later I emerged again from sleep
that seemed unsoiled, untroubled.
I stirred, turned on my side, felt a light breeze,
and opened fresher eyes to the brilliant day.
The sun rode high now and the song had ceased.
From near at hand, through the soft noonday hush,
I heard the gentle scuffling of the waves.

The wonder of the thing came over me:
what was this scene in which I found myself?
I got to my feet again and stared out seaward,
and saw far off beyond the watery dazzle
outlines of other islands, vague and still.
They seemed familiar, yet I could not place them.

I laughed to myself: I was lost.
And yet, being lost, I knew I had somehow arrived
at the place predestined and the time foretold.
The god stood by me still and I bowed to him,
and as I did, all at once the song was resumed—
not voiceless now, but fleshed in human tones.

The breeze blew fresh, and memories returned
of the man I had been in the days before the dream,
and tears poured down my cheeks as the song came closer.
I wept, and knew myself—and then I saw her,
white-robed and tall, walking the beach alone—
alone as every spirit is alone—
head thrown back, "trilling like a swan by Xanthos,"
that girl with splendid tawny hair . . .

AFTER SHEN ZHOU

A single chime of jade across the waters

as along this rocky shore the moment expands
and somewhere within it is hidden a dwelling apart
to which only the absolute ones make good their escape.

The Way seems not to exist (so the master taught)
and yet it is there—and springtime returns once more,
ageless and unreclaimed, to the inner lands.
What purity! The peach trees are in blossom,
birds chirp and stir, and there by the narrow stream
two white-robed figures wait to greet my crossing . . .

Shall I not make my move at last, and join them?

A NOTE ON THE AUTHOR

Frederick Morgan is a native New Yorker and graduate of Princeton University. During World War II he served in the Tank Destroyer Corps of the U.S. Army. A founder of *The Hudson Review* in 1947, he edited it for fifty years until the spring of 1998 and remains affiliated with it in his capacity as Founding Editor. Since 1998, the magazine has been edited by his wife, the art and architecture critic Paula Deitz. His poems have appeared in a wide variety of magazines and journals in the United States and abroad. He has published ten books of poems, two collections of prose fables, and two books of translations. In 1984 he was made Chevalier de l'Ordre des Arts et des Lettres by the government of France. In 2001 he was named winner of the Aiken Taylor Award for poetry.

Morgan spends most of his time in New York City, with summers in Blue Hill, Maine.

ACKNOWLEDGMENTS

The Introduction by Dana Gioia was originally
commissioned as an Aiken Taylor lecture and
delivered at the ceremony honoring the author
as the fifteenth Aiken Taylor poet, University
of the South, December 2001.

The poems in this book first appeared (sometimes
in earlier versions) in the following publications:

The American Scholar

The Hudson Review

The New Criterion

Northeast Corridor

Pivot

Poetry

The Poetry Review

The Sewanee Review

The Southern Review

Tar River Poetry

The Texas Review

Grateful acknowledgment is made to the Editors.
Particular thanks to Michael Peich for his
masterful Aralia Press editions of "The Christmas
Tree," "After Shen Zhou" and "Washington
Square." Thanks also to Ron Koury, Emily
Montjoy and Jon Mooallem for their help in
assembling this collection.